Dust Devils Dancing

A Haiku Anthology

edited by Margaret Tims with contributions
from members of Ver Poets

BRENTHAM PRESS

THE HAIKU is a strange little three-legged beast, originally from Japan, which hops along on lines of 5-7-5 syllables.

The traditional Japanese haiku was concerned with nature and the seasons. The English-language version, as practised now in Britain and America, may include a wider view of human nature with elements of irony, pathos or humour. Variations in structure have also crept in, but here the classical form is adhered to.

Essentially, the haiku is a paradox in which the moment of recognition is captured and held for scrutiny like a butterfly on a pin.

First published 1997 by
Brentham Press - 40 Oswald Road - St Albans - Herts AL1 3AQ

ISBN 0 905772 53 9

British Library Cataloguing-in-Publication Data:
A catalogue record for this book is available from the British Library

Design and printing by Melody, 4 Gainsborough Avenue, St Albans

The moon is tangled
in branches, but a walk in
the field sets it free.

The moon and this star -
are they inches apart or
would you say, miles... years ?

Leaves of the thistle
clamped to earth, radiating
like points of a star.

On to mid-April,
walking over grass grown thick
as a young girl's hair.

Bright water birds drift
into the sun, blind the eyes
become silhouettes.

When the water is
glass and only I watch, then
a heron appears.

A cricket match played
under black cloud, the whiteness
becoming intense.

A wet umbrella
placed out of doors just beyond
the reach of the rain.

Someone quietly
singing in the bathroom, of
his sins forgiven.

The towel hung out
to dry, found in the evening
upon the damp grass.

Wind through marram grass
harsh cry of gannet soaring
midsummer sea shore.

White tissue paper
sailing the soft night breeze
a mute swan swimming.

Dark snow clouds looming
flurries of small birds flying
dead leaves blown skyward.

Soft night rain falling
wind rustling dead autumn leaves
old secret whispered.

In frozen winter
  frosted slender holly trees
  green hands clasped in prayer.

Marks of tail, of feet
    woodmouse traced in frozen snow
    winter's calling card.

Icicles gleaming
  hang from steepest cottage roof
  midwinter fingers.

Unknown voices call
  unheard through dark curtain
  grief enters quickly.

Dust devils dancing
across the thirsting prairie
before summer rains.

The cicadas sing
during the heat of the day
tuning their back legs.

I'm a grain of salt
washed by the tropical rain
to live or dissolve ?

The set aside field
flowers at all times of year
home to butterflies.

The Painted Lady
flies from Africa in spring
to land on thistles.

Next-door neighbour's dog
steals the fox's meal and chokes
on a chicken bone.

The washing machine
becomes home to the badger
who comes out cleaner.

She drives to Cornwall
through the middle of the night
in most dense traffic.

The fisherman's boat
is a mere reflection
of the black-tailed fish.

Those who go before
get to their destination
later than they think.

For ever, you said
 holding the hand that still waits
 for your longed-for touch.

Touch, a language
without words, exploring the
syntax of desire.

The small white dog, curled
 like a netsuke, makes a
 life-art from sleeping.

Spring, the breeze fingers
 the knickers and nylons on
 the orchard wash line.

Like the warm russet
of the redwing on our birch
love lights up winter.

The honk of geese flies
above us; the whirring wings
fill empty twilight.

White water lilies
growing inside a glass house:
light invades winter.

The office looks on
this pool: water flows through stones
and makes a fountain.

A tree on the wall:
  its branches are sharp, perfect –
  it is a shadow.

Looking from our house
  together we see blue sky
  through trees' bare branches.

The whole sun held by
  trees reflectd in water
  is tamed at our feet.

Like fossil microbes
  from Mars, everything he says
  has to be questioned.

Fog hangs heavy yet
a blackbird sings, knowing of
a brilliant dawn.

By the pebbled pool
she says see my frog ! – we look
where a frog might be.

Mailed fist of sound
insulting the town, two wheels
overtake the queue.

With Radio three
chasing thoughts with classic jazz
J try to haiku.

J drank in your smile
when J touched your breasts but oh !
that gift of a kiss.

Present to a child:
bright paper, a ribboned bow
but an empty box.

Travelling by night
leads to the morning. To gain
the gift of the sun.

J have reached my home.
The sun shines on the windows
but who has locked the door ?

Robin on a spade -
someone is digging again
in the old garden.

The fox finds a track
under gooseberry bushes
green and full of spines.

After the blossom
of the early white blackthorn
comes the bitter sloe.

Slugs hole strawberries
thrushes strip currant bushes
high summer is come.

Down the well-known lane
stirring drifts of fallen leaves
mother and father.

Snow on the stone wall
frost on the twigs and branches
winter's white lilac.

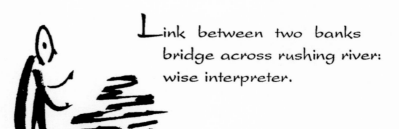

Link between two banks
bridge across rushing river:
wise interpreter.

Mighty elephant
double-decker of the plains
swerves from mini-mouse.

The high-rise giraffe
cranes through the neighbours' curtains
in the canopy.

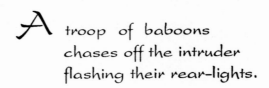

A troop of baboons
chases off the intruder
flashing their rear-lights.

Monarch of the glen,
the stag at bay is ransom'd
by the saboteurs.

Endangered species:
avarice puts out the light
of Blake's bright tiger.

A grinding of gears ...
traffic deadens the senses.
The cat's whiskers twitch.

Time's clock ticks faster
as each year accelerates.
How slowly he walks.

Ash sprinkled on earth
signals the passing of life
and feeds a new root.

We come into life
with the first breath and go out
in a puff of smoke.

The snow so lovely
  white fluffy and enticing
  turns us upside down.

For democracy,
  the gap is growing wider
  between poor and rich.

Ideas transferred
  direct to words on paper
  impress more deeply.

Peter Williamson

A waddle of crows
in a St Martin's summer:
can winter be near ?

Ringing the changes
hickory trees turn to gold
leave us astonished.

The squirrel steals nuts
from birds hunted by the cat
how can the bird win ?

The head of the thrush
turns sideways and slants so he
can listen for worms.

The cat asleep by
the pond's edge hears a small plop
but he is too late.

Redwings carry joy
our winter is their summer.
Look back when spring comes.

Vivaldi taught joy
to orphan girls in Venice
which lives with us still.

Walking through arches
we hear the ancient music,
leave - but remember.

THE CONTRIBUTORS

---

also from Brentham Press

VER POETS' VOICES

Thirtieth anniversary anthology, edited by May Badman and Margaret Tims, with contributions from around eighty members of this respected poetry group. The selection includes both established and aspiring writers, all dedicated to furthering the art of poetry.

ISBN 0 905772 48 2
112 pages   £6.95

available at local bookshops or post-free from the publisher

Brentham Press
40 Oswald Road
St Albans
Herts AL1 3AQ

Dust devils dancing
across the thirsting prairie
before summer rains.

Just one from this miscellaneous collection of Japanese-style Haiku, a
three-line verse form concerned with the elements, the natural world
and human responses.

The contributors are all members of Ver Poets.

Edited and illustrated by Margaret Tims

Brentham Press
St Albans

ISBN 0 905772 53 9

Price in UK £3.00